T0017554

Pavla Hanáčková & Mária Nerádová

HOW KIDS CELEBRATE CHRISTMAS AROUND THE WORLD

ALBATROS

Discover Christmas in:

Everyone loves Christmas!

The smell of sweets and cakes all around, Christmas music filling the air, the whole house beautifully decorated, yummy treats being baked, and everyone looking forward to giving and receiving gifts. Have you ever wondered how Christmas is celebrated elsewhere in the world? Because although it is celebrated practically everywhere, each place is different. In some countries, for instance, children unwrap their presents in December, while others do so in January. In some countries Christmas is celebrated mainly for religious reasons, while in others it is more of a secular event.

Have you ever heard of the *kallikantzari*? And do you know who brings presents to children in Finland? What is *pan de jamón*? Where can people sunbathe and swim in the sea on Christmas Day?

What's the same everywhere is that Christmas gives people the opportunity to spend quality time with their nearest and dearest. And isn't that the nicest gift that Christmas can give?

Get ready to learn tons of interesting new things. Just look into the magic glass globe to see how Christmas is celebrated all over the world. It will take you wherever you want to go! The Christmas globe, if you look closely enough, is hidden in every picture. Can you find it? If you can, it will take you to the next place.

Christmas in Spain

In Spain, a nationwide Christmas lottery is held every year on December 22nd—with the winners winning big! On Christmas Eve—known as *Nochebuena*—the whole family then meets for a feast that includes seafood or meat and lots of sweet things, too. Christmas is a time for family, and children have to wait for their presents until Epiphany (January 6th). So that they aren't sorry for the long wait, **Papá Noel** (the Spanish name for Santa Claus) leaves them a few small presents under the tree, and they open these the following morning. After dinner, it is common for Spaniards to visit their friends to wish them a Merry Christmas. Every home has a Christmas tree and a nativity scene. In Catalonia "El Caganer"—a naughty yet celebratory character from their local folklore—is added to the nativity scene. This mischievous figure is of a boy taking a poop—symbolizing good fortune and a good harvest! Catalanian homes also have a Yule log on display.

Christmas
in Germany

It is unthinkable that a German family should celebrate Christmas without a tree. After all, Germany is where Christmas trees first started! Originally they were decorated mainly with apples, nuts, and dried fruit. Every home also has an Advent wreath and an Advent calendar, on which children count off the days until Christmas. Christmas markets are held in practically every German town. Here

Germans can buy stollen sweet bread, gingerbread, and hot punch, and there are fairground rides and figures of the Nutcracker. Christmas here is celebrated on December 24th, when a traditional dinner is followed by gift-giving from the **Christkind** (an angelic figure who visits the south of the country) and the **Weihnachtsmann** (Santa Claus, who visits the north).

Christmas in Mexico

Here the celebration of Christmas is like a carnival—it is filled with color, laughter, and children's games. Many festivities are held throughout the Christmas holidays, known as *Las Posadas*. Nativity scenes are everywhere. Alongside the traditional figures, these scenes contain typical Mexican elements, such as flamingos and prickly pears. People visit their friends and attend mass, and children play games. One of the most popular activities is the smashing of the piñata. Presents are brought on Christmas Eve by **Santo Clos**, and children unwrap them at the stroke of midnight.

Typical Mexican Christmas decorations include the poinsettia, a flower known as the **'Christmas Star.'**

The piñata is made of papier-mâché and is filled with all kinds of sweets, which spill out when it breaks. Christmas piñatas are spherical in shape and have seven points, representing the seven deadly sins.

There is so much good food at Christmas dinner. **Traditional dishes** include roast suckling pig or turkey, tamales (corn-based dough with a filling, wrapped in a corn husk), and a special Christmas fruit salad.

Christmas in the USA

Christmas traditions here are as diverse as the people, varying from family to family. For everyone, though, Christmas is filled with merriment. On Christmas Eve (December 24th) family members come together to decorate the Christmas tree at home, often singing carols. Everyone looks forward to the Christmas dinner, which often includes roast turkey and vegetables, potatoes, cranberry sauce, and cake. After dinner the children hang stockings from the mantelpiece—if they have been good all year long, **Santa Claus** will fill these with presents. First thing on Christmas morning (December 25th), still in their pajamas, they run to the tree to see what Santa has left them.

Every Christmas Eve, Santa goes out on his sleigh, which is pulled by nine reindeer, to deliver presents to all the children of the world. He often enters people's homes by the **chimney**, landing in the fireplace.

As Santa has so many presents to deliver in a single night, next to their stockings the children leave **cookies and milk for him, and carrots for his reindeer**, so they can keep up their strength.

For Christmas, most American homes are decorated, and there are lights everywhere. Sometimes neighbors compete to see who has the most beautiful **decorations**.

Christmas in Japan

The Japanese have imported Christmas from the West and adapted it in their own image. Young lovers here see Christmas as a day for romance—they go to restaurants, where they eat strawberry cake, give each other presents, and declare their love for each other. The restaurants decorate Christmas trees with origami ornaments. And Japanese children enjoy Christmas, too. They decorate the tree at home, have a Christmas Eve dinner with their parents, and **Santa Claus** brings them presents in the night.

Strawberry cake is typical of the Japanese Christmas. Families bake it at home or buy it in a shop. It is decorated with whipped cream and fresh strawberries—its white and red colors are reminiscent of Christmas.

Families gather for the Christmas Eve dinner, for which the moms prepare **grilled or fried chicken.** There is even a special Christmas cake for dessert!

In Japan, Santa Claus doesn't leave the children's presents under the tree. Instead, he leaves them on the bed, **next to the pillow**. On Christmas morning, children can unwrap their presents without even having to get up!

Christmas in Australia & New Zealand

FRESH JUICE!

hello baby

Christmas "down under" has many similarities with Christmas in the USA or Britain. The big difference is, here it's the height of summer, and many people spend Christmas Day at the beach, enjoying the sun. Because of the heat, some prefer a lighter meal to the traditional turkey. **Santa Claus** puts presents under the tree, and the children unwrap them on the morning of December 25th. Here in Australia, though, Santa's sleigh is sometimes pulled by kangaroos rather than reindeer, which aren't used to the summer weather. New Zealanders celebrate in a very similar way, with one peculiarity. Their local symbol for Christmas is the pōhutukawa tree, whose red flowers are sometimes included in holiday decorations.

Christmas in Greece

Although the Greek Christmas has typical features of its own, it has embraced many customs from other countries. On December 24th it is traditional for children to go from house to house, bringing good wishes and singing carols. In the evening all family members come together for the Christmas feast, after which they attend Midnight Mass. Although Christmas is celebrated in December and the children of some families open their presents at this time, tradition states that gifts are brought by **Agios Vasilis**, an old man in a red-and-white suit, on New Year's Eve.

Everyone looks forward to the **Christmas feast**, because it is preceded by a fast that lasts 40 days. It includes roast turkey and stuffing, beautifully decorated *Christopsomo* (Christ's bread), and other sweet things, most notably honey cookies filled with walnuts and almond cookies dusted with powdered sugar.

According to Greek legend, **trouble-making goblins** called *kallikantzari* surface from the earth for the twelve days of Christmas. They enter people's homes through the fireplace and get up to all kinds of mischief. One way of chasing them away is to keep a fire burning in the hearth.

Long ago, during Christmas, the Greeks didn't decorate trees—instead, their tradition was to decorate **boats**. In switching over to trees they have followed the lead of other countries. At Christmas time today, **trees** (many of them artificial) are seen practically everywhere in Greece.

Christmas in Ethiopia

As Ethiopians use the Julian calendar—which is like a regular calendar, only its dates are nearly two weeks ahead—Christmas is celebrated here on January 7th. Ethiopians go to church in the early morning. This is followed by the feast and family celebration. There is no Christmas tree here, and only small presents are given. The most important thing is to spend time with family and friends. They also have a lot of fun playing a game called *ganna*, which is similar to field hockey!

Traditional dishes, for instance different kinds of meat with sauces and vegetables, are served at the Christmas feast. People pick up their food with a flatbread called *injera*, which serves as both plate and cutlery.

As Christmas is a religious festival, people pray a lot at this time. They get up for church before four in the morning, and the Mass can last for over three hours.

Although Ethiopians give each other only **small presents**, they take great pleasure in them. Children receive new festive clothes, for instance.

Christmas in Italy

The towns are filled with lights, the Christmas markets are buzzing with life, and homes are decorated with beautiful Christmas trees and nativity scenes. On Christmas Eve, families go to church together, and the next day, after the Pope has given his yearly address to the City of Rome and the world, the family starts its celebration.

Everyone meets for a lavish meal, which includes a sweet bread called *panettone*. Two figures bring presents to the children: it is traditional for the kindly witch **Befana** to do so on Epiphany Eve (January 5th). These days she is helped, in December, by **Babbo Natale** (Italy's name for Santa Claus).

24.12.

5.1.

LEO MIA

21

Christmas in Israel

Here in Israel they have Jewish synagogues, Muslim mosques, and Christian churches. Christmas is important for Christians, and here they celebrate it in style. The main celebrations in Israel take place in Bethlehem, where Jesus was born, and Nazareth, where he grew up. Worshipers come here from all over the world, and they can watch church services on huge screens in the squares. On Christmas Day in Bethlehem, parades of scout bands and school groups are held. Israeli children receive presents from Santa Claus, who is known as **Baba Noel.**

The food served on Christmas Eve depends on where the family is from and/or their faith. Some favor turkey, others lamb with rice.

Jesus Christ was born in Bethlehem. The site of his birth is marked with a fourteen-point silver star on a marble floor of the grotto above which the Church of the Nativity was built. This is a place of pilgrimage for the faithful.

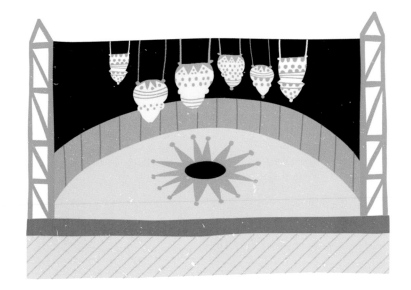

Christmas in Russia

Here the Orthodox Christmas is a largely religious festival that is celebrated on January 7th. The date is later because Russia uses the Julian calendar. On the night of their Christmas Eve (January 6th) people attend the divine liturgy in church. On returning home, they sit down to a lavish dinner, which everyone greatly looks forward to, as Christmas is preceded by a forty-day fast. Children are given presents not on Christmas but on New Year's Day (January 1st)—by **Ded Moroz** (Grandfather Frost) and his assistant the Snow Maiden.

Christmas in Venezuela

Venezuelan Christmas is filled with color, music, and fun. People leave their homes before dawn to attend church. Car-driving is forbidden, so people travel to church on roller skates! Christmas Carols fill the air, and everything is beautifully illuminated by fireworks. Those who fear they might oversleep tie one end of a length of string to their big toe and dangle the other from their window. Passing skaters can give this a tug to wake the sleeper. On Christmas Eve, another great Mass is celebrated, and afterward families sit down at a sumptuously laid table to give thanks for an exceptional evening.

Typical foods include:
- baked ham
- *pan de jamón* (a savory roll with ham and olives)
- *hallaca* (corn-based dough with a filling, wrapped in a banana leaf).
- *dulche de lechoza* (a sweet dessert made of papaya)

Presents are brought by **El Niño Jesus** at midnight. They are unwrapped under the tree on Christmas Day.

Some homes have a decorated Christmas tree, although small **nativity scenes**—known as *pesebres*—are more typical.

Christmas in Finland

Joulupukki

Finland

Lapland

Finnish children don't need to worry that they won't get any gifts, as gifts are brought on Christmas Eve by **Joulupukki** (the Finnish name for Santa Claus), who lives practically around the corner—in Lapland, near the Arctic Circle, where his workshop is located and the elves help him make the presents. Joulupukki is an old man with a white beard, dressed in red and white and holding a walking stick.

Before the children receive their presents, they manage to do many things—take a sauna, feed the birds, and perhaps go to the cemetery to light a candle for the departed. After that, the whole family gathers for a lavish dinner.

Christmas in France

As adults normally work during the day, Christmas celebrations in France don't begin until the early evening of Christmas Eve. Most homes have a decorated Christmas tree and a nativity scene. The whole family attends midnight Mass and then hurries home to a spectacular dinner.

The main course is roast turkey, and a typical dessert is a chocolate yule log called *bûche de Noël*. Homes are visited at night by **Père Noël** (Father Christmas), who resembles Santa. The presents he leaves under the tree are unwrapped in the morning.

How Kids Celebrate Christmas Around the World

Author: Pavla Hanáčková
Theme: Karolina Medková
Illustrations © Mária Nerádová, 2016

© B4U Publishing for Albatros,
an imprint of Albatros Media Group, 2021.
5. května 1746/22, Prague 4, Czech Republic.
Printed in China by Leo Paper Group.
ISBN: 978-80-00-06131-3

All rights reserved. Reproduction of any content
is strictly prohibited without the written permission
of the rights holders.

www.albatrosbooks.com